For Your Wedding
D R E S S E S

For Your Wedding

D R E S S E S

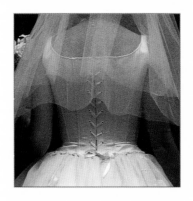

Tracy Guth

FRIEDMAN/FAIRFAX
P U B L I S H E R S

A FRIEDMAN/FAIRFAX BOOK

© 2000 by Michael Friedman Publishing Group, Inc.

Library of Congress Cataloging-in-Publication Data available upon request.

ISBN 1-56799-809-7

Editor: Ann Kirby
Art Director: Jeff Batzli
Designer: Stephanie Bart-Horvath
Photography Editors: Amy Talluto/Erin Feller
Production Manager: Ingrid McNamara

Color separations by Colourscan Overseas Co Pte Ltd
Printed in Hong Kong by C&C Offset Printing Co., Ltd.

1 3 5 7 9 10 8 6 4 2

For bulk purchases and special sales, please contact:
Friedman/Fairfax Publishers
Attention: Sales Department
15 West 26th Street
New York, New York 10010
212/685-6610   FAX 212/685-1307

Visit our website:
www.metrobooks.com

Front cover photograph ©Kamron Hinatsu

CONTENTS

INTRODUCTION

*W*edding lore has it that a bride should not let her groom see her in her dress—or even see the dress itself—before the big day. Why? The answer has to do with superstition and leftover ritual from the days of arranged marriages, but there's also the fact that this is quite possibly the most important, intricate, and beautiful dress you'll ever wear, and you want the first moment he sees you in it to be wonderfully memorable.

A wedding dress transforms a harried, stressed-out engaged woman into a serene, gorgeous bride. Whether you choose a full ball gown created out of miles of tulle and lace or a simple white satin sheath dress without much adornment at all, this piece of clothing should make you feel transformed, confident, positively blissful. It's a tall order, but wedding gowns manage to do just that. The instant you pull the right one over your head, the second its curves hug yours, you just know.

PAGE 6: HALTER NECKLINES CAN MAKE FOR STUNNING BACK DETAILS. WIDE SILK BANDS CREATE A DRAMATIC IMPRESSION ON THIS MANALÉ DRESS, AND LAYERS OF VEILING EMPHASIZE THE LUSH USE OF MATERIAL.

OPPOSITE: WITH A DISTINCTLY GRECIAN FEEL, THIS SILK AND COTTON GABARDINE DESIGN BY LILA BROUDE RESEMBLES A WHITE MARBLE COLUMN IN ITS SILKY SIMPLICITY. BEADWORK OF SILK FLOSS AND SILK ROSEBUDS, ALONG WITH TINY AUSTRIAN CRYSTALS, DEFINE THE STRAPS AND NATURAL WAIST. A CRISP SQUARE NECKLINE IS THE PERFECT CHOICE.

The wearing of white dates back to ancient Greece and Rome. For both civilizations white was symbolic of joy and celebration, as well as a repellant to evil spirits, and so brides donned it to wed. Ancient Greek brides also wore flame-yellow veils and sandals, in honor of Hymen, the god of marriage. But plenty of other hues have been bridal. Red has long been a popular wedding color, preferred in the Middle Ages and still the lucky, joyful shade worn by Chinese, Hindu, and Islamic brides. In Korea yellow and red are wedding colors. In Russia the traditional wedding hue is blue, a color also worn to trim the white gowns of ancient Hebrew brides. Until the mid-twentieth century, Icelandic brides favored black velvet gowns with metallic detailing, and in some regions of Spain, Roman Catholic brides still wear ornate black lace wedding dresses.

In early nineteenth-century Europe, women simply wore their best dress to marry; commoners often donned something blue, and royals always married in silver. Likewise, in the New World brides simply wore the best dress they could afford, and that often meant a white linen shift over a petticoat, a blue and white frock with a lace apron over it, or something in pink with velvet trim. During the Revolutionary War, American brides considered it patriotic to wear red, symbolizing the Colonies' drive for independence, and during the Civil War brides wore purple, the color of virtue and valor, to honor the war dead. In general, only members of the most privileged classes owned white gowns, because they could only be worn a few times before they were soiled. (There was no dry cleaning back then!)

It wasn't until Queen Victoria—who, indeed, completely defined her era—wore white in 1840 to wed her beloved Prince Albert that white truly became the

OPPOSITE: A STUNNING BOW MARKS THE MEETING PLACE BETWEEN A BEADED, LOW-BACKED BODICE AND A TRADITIONAL TRAIN, ENSURING AN ELEGANT EXIT FOR ANY BRIDE.

ultimate bridal color. From that point, it connoted the purity of the bride, and that symbolism was to stick for a long time. The veil also symbolizes this modesty and purity; its roots can be traced to the days of matchmaking, when the couple was not to see each other at all during (and sometimes even before) the wedding—the bride was always to be veiled, until the moment the couple said their vows. George Washington's stepdaughter Nellie Custis usually gets credit for popularizing the white-lace wedding veil; supposedly she was standing behind a lace window shade, and her fiancé proclaimed the sight so stunning that she chose to re-create the moment for their wedding.

These days, white is again the color of celebration—and no, you don't have to be a first-time bride to wear it. Plenty of remarrying women dress in white to celebrate their new beginning. Then again, many women choose another shade, whether this is their first marriage or not. Dress designers have taken to infusing dresses with color in the 1990s, from soft pastel underskirts to metallic embroidery, colored pearls, and faux jewels.

Your gown defines your wedding—or is defined by the wedding you've decided to have. An ultra-formal affair in an ornate ballroom calls for a completely different kind of dress than an intimate ceremony and family reception at your grandmother's rural country home. But whether you plan your wedding around the dress or match your gown to the vision of your day, it's important to focus on this important purchase early. You'll want to start shopping for your gown at least nine months before your wedding day; a year is not too early. This will give you plenty of time to shop, to allow time for the store that orders your chosen dream

dress to receive it, and then for you to have two or three fittings, so that you'll fit into your gown as if it were a second skin.

Shopping for your gown is a unique experience. If you choose to shop in a bridal salon, be sure to schedule an appointment so you'll get personalized service. It's also a good idea to try to shop on off-hours. Weekdays are your best bet; Saturday can be a nightmare, with countless brides clamoring for dresses. Don't bring too many fellow shoppers along or you may feel overwhelmed; Mom, your sister, and/or your maid of honor will do.

Generally a salon will assign you a bridal consultant, who will help you navigate your way through the multitude of dresses available. You may or may not be able to look through the gowns on your own; based on what you say you're looking for, or photographs of dresses you like, your consultant will bring you gowns to try on. If you purchase your dress at the salon, you will likely keep working with this same person throughout your fittings and until the dress is ready.

You can also search for a dress in a bridal outlet or warehouse. This is more like traditional shopping, with rows and rows of wedding gowns available for you to browse. For other options, consider having your dream dress custom-made by a seamstress, or wear your mother's or grandmother's wedding gown. It may need to be restored or altered, but what a wonderful symbolic gesture.

Needless to say, there are thousands of styles to choose from. It helps to have a little background before you jump into shopping for "The Dress." In the following pages, we'll examine the options, from silhouettes to fabric and color, to help you find the gown that's just right for you.

OPPOSITE: THE BODICE OF YOUR DRESS SHOULD BE EQUALLY SPECIAL VIEWED FROM FRONT OR BACK. GEOMETRIC CUT-OUTS, EMBROIDERY, AND BOWS ARE ALL GORGEOUS OPTIONS. WEARKSTATT'S NEW YORK CITY STORE SHOWS OFF A VARIETY OF UNIQUELY ARCHITECTURAL GOWNS.

CHAPTER ONE

SILHOUETTES

*T*he most important aspect of any dress is, of course, its shape. You may already

have an idea of which silhouettes you like, from a full ball gown to a narrow, sleek

sheath. Or perhaps your eye is drawn to the Empire period look, or the classic,

looks-great-on-everyone princess cut.

Whatever your fancy, as you'll soon find out, the best way to find the dress style

for you is to start trying them on. You might love how something looks in a picture

RIGHT: THE SIMPLE, SEAMLESS,
CLASSIC SHAPE OF AN A-LINE
(PRINCESS) SILHOUETTE
FLATTERS EVERY BRIDE. THIS
DUCHESSE-SATIN GOWN BY
AMSALE FEATURES A SCOOPED
HALTER NECKLINE, PEARL-
BEADED LACE AT THE HEM,
AND A CATHEDRAL TRAIN.
A BIT LESS FULL THAN A BALL
GOWN, AN A-LINE DRESS STILL
OFFERS THE LONG CIRCLE-SKIRT
EFFECT MANY WOMEN CRAVE
FOR THEIR WEDDING.

OPPOSITE: THE LOW SCOOP
NECKLINE OF THIS MANALÉ
DESIGN IS A CLASSIC, WITH
ITS THIN BORDER OF ROLLED
SILK THAT CONTINUES UP
ONTO THE SPAGHETTI STRAPS.
THIS NECKLINE CAN'T HELP
BUT FLATTER VIRTUALLY
EVERY BRIDE.

on a model, but when you see it on yourself, you may wonder just what you were thinking. Remember, too, that while you may already know what type of suit or cocktail dress flatters you best, shopping for a wedding gown is a whole different experience. Keep an open mind, and you may be pleasantly surprised!

You'll encounter various silhouettes, some of which look better on certain body types than on others. Here is a guide to the basic dress silhouettes.

(continued on page 24)

THE HIGH SHEEN OF THE BALL
GOWN SKIRT ON THIS MANALÉ
DRESS IS JUXTAPOSED WITH A
MORE MATTE BODICE, COVERED
WITH SUBTLE EMBROIDERY. THE
OVERALL EFFECT IS PURE,
UNDERSTATED GLAMOUR.

A CLASSIC COMBINATION: A
SIMPLE, FITTED SILK SATIN
BODICE IS PAIRED WITH A FULL
ORGANZA SKIRT ON THIS BALL
GOWN BY MANALÉ. FEEL FREE
TO PLAY WITH FABRICS—MIX-
ING AND MATCHING THEM IS
ESPECIALLY EASY ON SUCH AN
UNADORNED DRESS.

RIGHT: THIS SOFT, FLOWING
GOWN FEATURES DELICATE,
SHEER LONG SLEEVES WITH A
MATCHING SUBTLY SWAYING
TRAIN. THE BACK IS LEFT
BEAUTIFULLY BARE.

OPPOSITE: SATIN RIBBON
LACED THROUGH THE
BACK OF THIS BALL GOWN
TAKES THE PLACE OF MORE
TRADITIONAL BUTTONS OR
A LESS ATTRACTIVE ZIPPER.
SUCH DETAILING PROVIDES
SIMPLE GOWNS WITH A BIT
OF ORIGINALITY.

RIGHT: PETTICOATS AND
CRINOLINES CAN CREATE A
HOOP-SKIRT EFFECT, MAKING A
BALL GOWN THAT MUCH MORE
SPECIAL AND BRIDAL. YOU MAY
BE SURPRISED BY THE FEELINGS
THAT DIFFERENT SILHOUETTES
EVOKE IN YOU. EVEN IF YOU
THOUGHT SUCH A FULL
DRESS WASN'T YOUR STYLE,
TRYING ONE ON CAN BE A
TRANSFORMING EXPERIENCE.

OPPOSITE: THIS INCREDIBLE
THAI SILK BALL GOWN,
DESIGNED BY RANI FOR
ST. PUCCHI, WOULD TRULY
MAKE A BRIDE THE BELLE OF
THE BALL. IT'S ABSOLUTELY
FIT FOR A QUEEN, WITH
ITS PORTRAIT COLLAR,
CORSET BODICE, HAND
EMBROIDERY, AND THE
DESIGNER'S SIGNATURE
SWIRL BUSTLE.

Ball gown: This is the "Cinderella" wedding dress, with a fitted bodice, natural or dropped waist, and a full skirt, often made of organza or tulle, or in silk or satin with a full underskirt. You might choose a ball gown with a Basque waist, which involves a triangular design on the front waist of the dress. Ball gowns are flattering to many body types. A Basque waist beautifully hides full hips and thighs, if you're self-conscious, but this traditional shape can also lend some curves to a straight, boyish figure.

(continued on page 28)

OPPOSITE: MANALÉ'S SLEEVE-
LESS SILK CHIFFON AND SILK
SATIN SHEATH DRESS IS TRANS-
FORMED INTO A BALL GOWN
WITH A FULL, DETACHABLE
TRAIN. PRETTY BEADING AND
A SHAPELY V-BACKED BODICE,
JUXTAPOSED WITH A LINE OF
ELEGANT BACK BUTTONS ON
THE TRAIN ITSELF, CREATE A
TWO-PIECE CORSET-AND-SKIRT
EFFECT.

LEFT: THIS FASHION-FORWARD,
MINIMALIST BALL GOWN FROM
THE JADE DANIELS COLLECTION
IS A PERFECT EXAMPLE OF HOW
A FULL SKIRT ADDS CURVES TO
A BOYISH FIGURE. A SIMPLE,
UNADORNED SATIN BODICE
WITH A HIGH, HALTER-STYLE
NECKLINE FALLS RIGHT TO
THE HIPS; THE FULL ORGANZA
SKIRT CREATES A DRAMATIC
CONTRAST.

THE SLIGHTLY MODIFIED SCOOP NECKLINE ON THIS GOWN BY ANA HERNANDEZ IS CUT STRAIGHT ACROSS, CURVING UP SLIGHTLY JUST BEFORE THE SHOULDERS TO CREATE AN ELEGANT, ROMANTIC LINE. PRETTY SHEER CAP SLEEVES BORDERED IN SILK ARE TOPPED WITH SWEET SPRIGS OF FABRIC FLOWERS.

WEDDING GOWNS COME IN ALL SHAPES AND STYLES, AND ALL FABRICS, AS WELL. DESIGNER YUMI KATSURA CREATED THIS PRETTY, TOTALLY WEARABLE SHEATH OF CREAM STRETCH CREPE. A HIGH NECKLINE, ASYMMETRICAL SEAMS, AND A SHEER, MINIMALLY BEADED BACK PANEL FINISH THIS FRESH, MODERN BRIDAL LOOK.

Sheath: You don't necessarily have to be model-slim to wear this long, straight, slim look, often designed without much embellishment. Sheaths are quite flattering on petite women, because their simplicity and unbroken lines create length. If you are short, you'll want to consider a dress with detailing around the neckline, to call attention upward to your blushing bridal face. After Carolyn Bessette, the bride of J.F.K., Jr., wore one in 1996, a lot of simple white or cream slip dresses have been taking the walk down the aisle, too.

(continued on page 34)

RIGHT: A SIMPLE A-LINE
DESIGN PUTS THE FOCUS ON
THE WAY THE FABRIC MOVES
WHEN THE BRIDE DOES.
COMFORT IS KEY, AND THE
BEAUTY OF THE FULLNESS AND
CRISPNESS OF WEDDING-GOWN
FABRIC IS THAT THE SHAPE
OF YOUR DRESS SPEAKS FOR
ITSELF—AND ENHANCES YOUR
SHAPE IN THE PRETTIEST WAY.

OPPOSITE: A SIMPLE SATIN
SHEATH BY CARMELA SUTERA
STANDS OUT WITH EYE-
CATCHING BACK DETAILS—
A SCULPTURAL SATIN TRAIN
AND AN EXQUISITELY BEADED
SILK ORGANZA ILLUSION PANEL.
ESPECIALLY IF YOU DECIDE ON
A MINIMAL FRONT, THINK OF
THE VIEW GUESTS WILL GET
WHEN YOU'RE STANDING
AT THE ALTAR.

OPPOSITE: AN ELEGANT BALL GOWN SKIRT APPEARS THOROUGHLY MODERN WHEN PAIRED WITH A SLEEVELESS, HIGH-NECKED BODICE. THIS CRISP, SIMPLE DESIGN LOOKS LIGHT AND SUMMERY DESPITE THE SHEER VOLUME OF FABRIC.

LEFT: A DRAMATIC SILHOUETTE—THE NATURAL LIGHT ILLUMINATING THIS CHIFFON EMPIRE-WAIST WEDDING DRESS PUTS ITS BODICE AND SKIRT EMBELLISHMENT INTO SHARP, GORGEOUS FOCUS. NOTICE THE WAY THE FABRIC FALLS GRACEFULLY DOWNWARD FROM RIGHT BELOW THE BUSTLINE, SKIMMING OVER THE WAIST AND HIPS.

OPPOSITE: THERE'S A
WEDDING DRESS TO MATCH
EVERY WOMAN'S STYLE.
THIS LONG-SLEEVED SILK
SATIN CREPE SHEATH IS FAR
FROM TRADITIONAL. ITS LEAN,
DRAMATIC SILHOUETTE IS
TAILORED AND SOPHISTICATED.
A MATCHING SILK CHIFFON VEIL
ECHOES THE DRESS ITSELF LIKE
AN ETHEREAL SHADOW.

Empire: A wonderful period look, this high-waisted dress with pretty bodice details was made popular again when Gwyneth Paltrow wore the style so charmingly in the 1996 movie *Emma.* Beneath the bustline the dress falls in a slight A-line to the floor. If you have an undefined waistline, this is a stylish cover-up, but if your hips and/or bust are full, this look may not work for you. It depends on the dress, though—if you love it, try it on.

Princess/A-line: This silhouette is probably the most popular, because almost any woman can wear it. There are no seams at the waist, and the skirt's line is triangular, for a smooth, elongated look through the torso. A princess dress is often more substantial and shaped than a sheath, it feels comfortable to women of various body shapes.

You'll also want to consider the type of train you want your dress to have, if any. The shortest train is called a sweep; it just touches the floor. The longest is a cathedral train—think Princess Diana on her wedding day, with all that frothy fabric flowing out behind her.

CHAPTER TWO

NECKLINES AND SLEEVES

PAGE 36: THE PORTRAIT NECKLINE IS A PERFECT WAY TO FRAME YOUR FACE. IT ALSO GIVES YOU THE BENEFIT OF AN OFF-THE-SHOULDER LOOK (SHOW OFF THAT DÉCOLLETAGE!) WHILE STILL HIDING YOUR UPPER ARMS, A COMFORTABLE STYLE FOR MANY WOMEN. THIS DRESS ALSO HAS A TINY SLEEVE FOR ADDED COVERAGE.

OPPOSITE: THE SCOOP NECKLINE ON THIS LONG-SLEEVED APPLIQUÉD DRESS IS ADORNED WITH A WREATH OF SILK ROSES, BEAUTIFULLY ECHOING THE PEACH FLOWERS IN THE BRIDE'S BOUQUET. HER MAID OF HONOR, AT RIGHT, WEARS A GOWN WITH A SIMILAR NECK, THIS ONE MADE OF DRAPED CHIFFON.

LEFT: A SQUARE NECKLINE AND THREE-QUARTER LENGTH SLEEVES LEND THIS ORNATE BEADED LACE GOWN A SLIGHTLY LESS FORMAL FLAIR.

*F*ar from minor details, the neckline and sleeve styles you select are defining elements of your dress. The neckline frames your face and can reveal the delicate beauty of collarbones or emphasize a swanlike neck. The sleeves you choose—from full-length to spaghetti strap or from loose and flowing to arm-hugging—further refine your style.

OPPOSITE: THE SIMPLEST OF
SIMPLE NECKLINES—A SWEETLY
CLEAN SQUARE WITH PRETTY,
THIN STRAPS—TOPS THE PEARL-
BEADED LACE BUSTIER BODICE
OF THIS SILK PEAU DE SOIE
A-LINE GOWN BY AMSALE.
IT'S AN ELEGANT LOOK THAT
EMPHASIZES THE UPPER BODY
AND FLATTERS A SMALL-CHESTED
FIGURE.

LEFT: A WIDE BAND OF SATIN
AT THE NECKLINE IS ALL THIS
SLEEK SHEATH BY ANA
HERNANDEZ NEEDS IN THE
WAY OF EXTRAS. A MATCHING
STOLE FURTHER ENHANCES
THE SOPHISTICATED STYLE.

WEDDING DRESS NECKLINES DON'T HAVE TO PLUNGE, BUT THAT DOESN'T MEAN YOU'LL LOOK TOTALLY COVERED UP EITHER. THIS SLEEVELESS T-SHIRT, OR JEWEL, NECKLINE IS UNDERSTATED AND ELEGANT IN A 1950s, AUDREY HEPBURN WAY.

THE HEART-SHAPED
SWEETHEART NECKLINE IS
LOVED BY COUNTLESS BRIDES
BECAUSE IT'S AN IDEAL
CLEAVAGE ENHANCER.
WOMEN WITH FULL BUSTS
SHOULD NOT SHY AWAY FROM
THIS STYLE—THEY'RE THE
ONES WHOM IT FLATTERS
MOST! THIS SILK-SHANTUNG
A-LINE DRESS BY PRISCILLA
OF BOSTON FEATURES A
SWEETHEART FRONT WITH
CAP SLEEVES; YOU'LL ALSO
SEE OFF-THE-SHOULDER
SWEETHEART NECKLINES.

NECKLINES

Off-the-shoulder: This popular neckline sits below the shoulders, with sleeves that cover part of the upper arm. Although it depends on your comfort level, most women wear it well. Especially when combined with a sweetheart shape (see below), it can create very attractive cleavage. This look is also a beautiful way to show off your collarbone. If you're uncomfortable about baring so much of your arms or chest, consider a portrait neckline, a variation with extra fabric framing the neck and shoulders.

Sweetheart: Similar in shape to the upper half of a heart, this neckline is very flattering for fuller-chested women. It's often embellished with an overlay of lace or another sheer material that comes up above the heart shape, giving you a little more coverage, and pretty detail to boot.

Sabrina: This shape gently follows the curve of your collarbone, almost to the tip of the shoulders—it's cut straight across, so less décolletage is showing. Think Audrey Hepburn—very glamorous, but not showy. Women who are less endowed on top generally look better in this neckline than do those with fuller bustlines.

Scoop: Think Jacqueline Kennedy Onassis. Many designers are—the scoop is a neckline you'll see everywhere. It's usually square with rounded edges or a variation on that shape, and often the scoop continues on the back of the dress. You'll see variations that are more square, or even in a V shape. Very elegant and very comfortable, the scoop is a universal flatterer.

(continued on page 52)

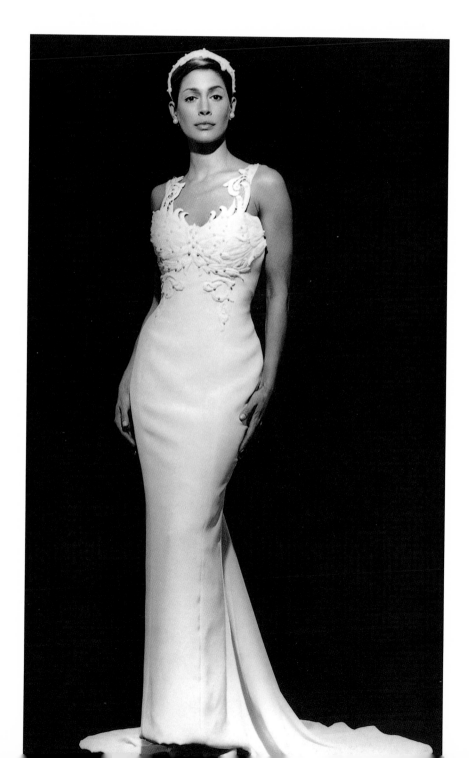

OPPOSITE: MANALÉ LAYERS A PERFECTLY HEART-SHAPED STRAPLESS SWEETHEART NECKLINE UNDER A SHEER "OVERBODICE" WITH JEWEL NECK AND LONG SLEEVES. THE LACE DESIGNS ON THE FULL SKIRT ARE ECHOED ON THE ILLUSION FABRIC, PULLING THE LOOK TOGETHER BEAUTIFULLY.

LEFT: HIGH FASHION MEETS BRIDAL TRADITION IN THIS SILK CREPE SHEATH ADORNED WITH THE JAPANESE COTTON APPLIQUÉS WITH PEARL BEADING THAT HAVE BECOME MIKA INATOME'S SIGNATURE DETAIL. A FISHTAIL TRAIN FURTHER ACCENTUATES AND CELEBRATES THIS BRIDE'S STUNNING CURVES.

RIGHT: THE SABRINA NECKLINE ON THIS SILK SATIN PRINCESS GOWN BY ULLA-MAIJA CUTS ALMOST STRAIGHT ACROSS THE DÉCOLLETAGE, SKIMMING THE COLLARBONE OUT TO THE TIPS OF THE SHOULDERS AND CREATING A SOFT, FEMININE LOOK. SMALLER-BUSTED WOMEN LOOK STUNNING IN THIS STYLE. THE UNIQUE GATHERED LAYERS GIVE A CONFECTIONARY SWIRL TO THE SKIRT.

OPPOSITE: THE PEARL AND CRYSTAL TRIM ON THE ALMOST-OFF-THE-SHOULDER NECKLINE OF THIS SILK SATIN BALL GOWN FACED WITH ORGANZA IS ECHOED AT THE DROPPED WAIST. BRIDES LOVE THIS SIMPLE YET VERY SPECIAL LOOK, AND DESIGNERS LIKE MANALÉ GIVE THEM FRESH AND LOVELY VERSIONS TO CHOOSE FROM.

OPPOSITE: DESIGNER VERA WANG PIONEERED THE USE OF "SHEER ILLUSION," THE SEE-THROUGH FABRIC SEEN ON THE ARMS, BACKS, AND NECKLINES OF COUNTLESS DESIGNERS DRESSES TODAY. HERE SHE USED SMALL TRIANGULAR PANELS WITH SILK BORDERS TO CREATE A PRETTY HALTER TOP FOR A FRESH TAKE ON THE CLASSIC BALL GOWN.

LEFT: THE "BIB"-STYLE BODICE—CUT HIGH AND SQUARE ACROSS THE CHEST, WITH TINY STRAPS—IS A TREND IN BRIDAL FASHION AND BEYOND. WEARKSTATT, A HUSBAND-AND-WIFE DESIGN TEAM, HAS INCORPORATED THE NECKLINE INTO THEIR SIGNATURE A-LINE LOOK, HERE ADDING FRENCH LACE ADORNED WITH BEADS, CRYSTALS, AND SEQUINS, PLUS PLATINUM DUCHESSE TRIM ON THE HEM AND STRAPS.

RIGHT: LOVE THE LOOK OF A JACKET OVER A SHELL? YOU CAN WEAR IT ON YOUR WEDDING DAY WITH A DRESS LIKE THIS ONE BY ANA HERNANDEZ. THE PRETTY LONG-SLEEVED JACKET, WITH ELEGANT LAPELS AND DELICATE CUFFS, CREATES A SLIMMING EFFECT AT THE WAIST (WITH THREE SATIN-COVERED BUTTONS) AND GIVES EXTRA COVERAGE WHILE REMAINING INCREDIBLY STYLISH.

OPPOSITE: THIS HIGH-NECKED FRENCH SILK SATIN GOWN BY MIKA INATOME CALLS TO MIND THE SPARE GLAMOUR OF THE 1940S. THE COLLAR AND CUFFS ARE HAND-RUCHED (THE MATERIAL HAS A GATHERED EFFECT), AND ONE HUNDRED BUTTONS LEAD TO A FISHTAIL TRAIN. AN UNEXPECTED, ELEGANT HEADPIECE COMPLETES THE LOOK.

Jewel: This neckline is similar to the look of a T-shirt; it's round and sits at the base of your throat. This is often a more conservative, covered-up look, but it's also a very simple, tailored style. Many full-figured women are attracted to this neckline as a way to downplay their bust, but it actually accentuates your chest—small-chested women might like it better.

Halter/High Neck: The cut-out halter shape, often with an open back, and the high-necked gown, often sleeveless, look best on a bride with broad shoulders and an athletic build. Also, the taller you are, the more flattering this might be.

SLEEVES

T-Shirt: This simple, familiar short sleeve is a good option for brides who want some sleeve coverage but don't want to go all the way to long.

Cap: Slightly shorter than T-shirt sleeves and often slightly rounded or scalloped, cap sleeves just cover the tops of your shoulders. They look best on women with fairly slender or well-toned upper arms.

Off-the-shoulder: This style covers the upper part of the arms while leaving the tops of the shoulders and décolletage exposed. Along with the off-the-shoulder neckline, this look accentuates cleavage and collarbone prettily, and generally covers enough of your arms to make you comfortable.

THE BACK OF THIS SILK-FACED
SATIN CHIFFON BALL GOWN
GETS A GARDEN FEEL FROM
PRETTY FLORAL EMBROIDERY,
WHICH ALSO DECORATES THE
LOWER SLEEVES. DESIGNER
MANALÉ LEFT THE FRONT OF
THE DRESS UNADORNED—
THIS IS ALL THE ADDED DETAIL
IT NEEDS.

Three-quarter: Echoing popular 1950s styles, three-quarter sleeves end midway between the elbow and the wrist for an elegant, sophisticated look.

Long sleeves: Simple and straight or full and lacy, long sleeve choices vary according to your desires: modesty, chilly temperatures, or simple taste will help you decide.

Spaghetti straps: Skinny straps expose your arms and shoulders; another option is to go strapless.

Sheer: Many dresses are available with sheer "illusion" sleeves, which vary in opacity from almost invisible to nearly opaque.

A HIGH NECKLINE AND CUT-AWAY SLEEVES ARE A GREAT WAY TO EXPOSE SEXY SHOULDERS WITHOUT GOING STRAPLESS.

EMBELLISHMENTS

*E*mbellishment is what sets a wedding dress apart from a basic long white dress. Designers make imaginative use of such elements as lace, beads, sequins, embroidery shot through with metallic thread, rhinestones, even faux jewels, feathers, or fur to adorn wedding dresses and make them truly unique.

It used to be that no wedding gown was complete without a sea of lacy frills and a bodice embedded with jewels—veritable bridal armor. You can certainly find such a dress, if that's your dream. But the trend today is toward elegant simplicity—

(continued on page 66)

RIGHT: AN ULTRA-FEMININE
RUFFLE ENCIRCLING THE
BIB BODICE MAKES THIS
VERA WANG BALL GOWN
FABULOUSLY FLIRTY. WRIST-
LENGTH GLOVES WITH
MATCHING CUFFS FINISH
THE EFFECT. NOTE THAT
THIS LOOK IS NOT AT ALL
CHILDISH; ON THE CONTRARY,
IT'S COMPLETELY GROWN-UP
AND MODERN.

OPPOSITE: THE OFF-THE-
SHOULDER EMBROIDERED
BODICE OF THIS JADE DANIELS
BALL GOWN SEEMS TO FLOAT IN
A SEA OF TULLE. THE BOUFFANT
SKIRT MATCHES THE BRIDE'S
FOUNTAIN VEIL, AND THE
OVERALL EFFECT IS DREAMY
WHILE AT THE SAME TIME
COMPLETELY SOPHISTICATED.

OPPOSITE: THE PAINSTAKING EMBROIDERY AND PEARLING ON THE BODICE AND SLEEVES OF THIS SILK SATIN DRESS IS THAT MUCH MORE STUNNING BECAUSE THE DESIGNER CHOSE TO CONTRAST THE COMPLEX DESIGN WITH A COMPLETELY UNADORNED SKIRT AND BUSTLE-TRAIN.

LEFT: FABULOUS DAISY-SHAPED APPLIQUÉS OUTLINE THE SCOOP NECK AND BACK (AND TINY PEARLS TRIM THE BASQUE WAIST) OF THIS OTHERWISE UNADORNED ALFRED SUNG GOWN. FLORAL EMBELLISHMENT LIKE THIS CAN BE PART OF A LARGER THEME; IMAGINE A DAISY-INSPIRED WEDDING, WITH DAISY BOUQUETS, DAISIES ON THE CAKE, DAISY CENTERPIECES—AND THIS DRESS.

RIGHT: DESIGNER MANALÉ
USES A TRELLIS-WEAVE
MATERIAL TO GIVE AN
OTHERWISE TRADITIONAL
GOWN A CRISP, COMPLETELY
ORIGINAL LOOK. THE
CONCEPT IS THE SAME AS
SHEER ILLUSION FABRIC,
BUT THE NEW, SURPRISING
TEXTURE IS TOTALLY FRESH.

less embellishment, but more time and care taken to create it. If the dress designer doesn't actually do this handwork personally, the company probably employs talented artisans in Europe. Much of the lace and embroidery you see on a custom-made wedding gown is done by hand, and most beads and jewels are not simply glued on in a manufacturer's factory; they are painstakingly placed and sewn. All this work creates a dress that's truly a work of art.

(continued on page 72)

LEFT: BRIDE TIMES TWO. THIS
ALFRED SUNG A-LINE GOWN
HAS AN HEIRLOOM-INSPIRED
BODICE MADE OF CROCHETED
LACE AND ADORNED WITH
PRETTY FLORAL APPLIQUÉS.
THE SIMPLE, FLOWY SKIRT
IS MADE OF CHIFFON, AN
UNUSUALLY LIGHT AND
EASY-TO-MOVE-IN MATERIAL.

OPPOSITE: DESIGNER CHRISTOS USED INTRICATE BANDS OF VENISE LACE TO MAKE THE BODICE OF THIS IVORY SILK DUPIONI GOWN AN ABSOLUTE WORK OF ART. HORIZONTAL PIECES GRACEFULLY NIP IN THE WAIST, CREATING A CORSET EFFECT; VERTICAL STRIPS FINISH WHAT COULD BE CONSIDERED A PERIOD LOOK.

LEFT: EVEN THOSE BRIDES WHO OPT FOR MOSTLY UNADORNED DRESSES CAN'T QUITE RESIST A FEW PRETTY EMBELLISHMENTS ON THE GOWN'S BACK. THIS SILK PEAU DE SOIE AMSALE GOWN FEATURES A TIERED BACK BUSTLE GATHERED WITH BLOOMING SILK FLOWERS.

OPPOSITE: WITH A CAP SLEEVE THERE'S JUST ENOUGH MATERIAL TO COVER YOUR SHOULDERS, LEAVING YOUR ARMS ELEGANTLY BARE, YET COMPLETELY COMFORTABLE. CAP SLEEVES LOOK WONDERFUL WITH A SLIGHTLY ROUNDED SQUARE NECKLINE, LIKE THAT OF THIS CHIFFON AND CREPE GOWN WITH BEADED VENISE-LACE BODICE BY EDEN BRIDALS.

LEFT: THIS LOW-CUT OFF-THE-SHOULDER NECKLINE IS EMBELLISHED WITH SILK-CHIFFON ROSES JUST UNDER THE SHOULDERS, WITH SIMPLE LONG SLEEVES BELOW. PAIRED WITH A MANTILLA VEIL, IT CREATES A STUNNING EFFECT INSPIRED BY NINETEENTH-CENTURY SPANISH BRIDES.

RIGHT: LEAVE IT TO INNOVATIVE DESIGNER MIKA INATOME TO CREATE A SILK SATIN SHEATH DRESS WITH STUNNING STERLING SILVER EMBROIDERY ON THE BODICE AND STERLING CHAINS ADORNING THE WAISTLINE. REST ASSURED YOU'LL STAND OUT IN SUCH A FABULOUS GOWN.

OPPOSITE: FABRIC ITSELF CAN BE USED AS EMBELLISHMENT. HERE, FIVE LARGE SATIN FLOWERS WITH TRAILING RIBBONS ADORN THE BACK WAIST OF A GOWN. JUST A TINY BIT OF THE BRIDE'S VEIL IS VISIBLE, BUT IT'S CLEAR THAT THE FLOWER FORMS SUBTLY ECHO THE FLOWING TULLE.

MIKA INATOME
NEW YORK
11 WORTH ST, RM 4B NEW YORK, NY 10013

Lace is a traditional wedding detail, and you can choose from various styles, named for the French and Italian towns where they were first created—Alençon, Chantilly, Venice. Their patterns are floral or geometric, with large, bold swirls or tiny, intricate stitching. Lace can adorn a bodice or create a band around the hem of a gown; you can wear lace gloves, or a veil with a matching lace pattern on its edges. Spanish brides wear all-lace veils called mantillas.

Embroidery is enjoying a renewed popularity—its intricate patterns can set off a neckline beautifully, or it can be used to decorate a waistline or a skirt. Designers often add subtle color to a gown by incorporating embroidered patterns, including gold and silver for a formal, festive feel. Beading is frequently worked right into the embroidery, giving it a textured, dimensional look.

THE BODICE OF THIS SILK SATIN
BALL GOWN BY ULLA-MAIJA
FEATURES PRETTY EMBROIDERY,
JUST ENOUGH TO COMPLEMENT
THE ELEGANT DRAPE OF A FULL
SKIRT. THE WIDE-BRIMMED HAT
TRIMMED WITH TULLE CREATES
A GLORIOUS FINISHING EFFECT.

Rhinestones, sequins, and other faux jewels are usually used sparingly—perhaps just to accent an embroidered design at the neckline with some additional color or sparkle, for instance. But some couture designers still use jewels to create wedding gowns reminiscent of their evening wear lines, and brides love them. You will probably also come across gowns fully ensheathed in sequins—and for the right bride at the right party, they can be spectacular. A long, detailed row of satin buttons is a beautiful back detail popular with many brides. And especially for fall and winter wedding dresses, it's becoming commonplace for designers to add a bit of faux fur at the neckline, hem, and/or cuffs to create a gorgeous seasonal look.

THE PETAL-THIN EDGE OF A WEDDING GOWN'S CHIFFON TRAIN, DECORATED WITH MINIATURE BUTTONS AND BOWS, PRACTICALLY BLENDS IN WITH THE REAL ROSE PETALS STREWN ON THE LAWN BENEATH THE BRIDE'S FEET.

CHAPTER FOUR

FABRIC
AND COLOR

PAGE 76: PASTELS, INCLUDING PINK, LAVENDER, AND PEACH, ARE THE HUES OF CHOICE FOR MOST WEDDING DRESS DESIGNERS VENTURING INTO COLOR. ULLA-MAIJIA CREATED THIS SENSATIONAL SHEATH IN A SHADE SHE CALLS "CLAY," A SOFT PINK-ORANGE COMBINATION.

OPPOSITE: THIS A-LINE GOWN WITH CRISSCROSS STRAPS IS MADE OF SILK MIKADO, A HEAVY SILK FAVORED BY THE DESIGNERS AT WEARKSTATT. THE PRETTY ORGANZA TRAIN IS DETACHABLE BUT ALSO SUPER-EASY TO BUSTLE, AS SHOWN HERE. GORGEOUS SILK FLOWER DETAILS FINISH THE LOOK.

LEFT: THE PRETTY HAND-STITCHED LACE PATTERN EMBEDDED IN THIS SHEER DRESS OVERLAY CREATES SUBTLE, BEAUTIFUL DETAIL OVER THE V-BACK OF A BRIDE'S GOWN. MANY OVERLAYS ARE SEPARATE PIECES; AFTER THE CEREMONY, YOU CAN REMOVE THE TOP LAYER AND WEAR JUST THE SHEATH TO THE RECEPTION.

*N*ow that you've thought about the details—the right shape and neckline, beautiful lace or embroidery—it's time to consider the fundamentals: the perfect fabric and the most flattering color. Silk and satin are the most traditional and popular fabrics, and they're often used in combination to give the dress shape and sheen. Silk is, of course, the most sought-after fabric for any type of dress, and it's no less in demand for wedding gowns.

(continued on page 29)

RIGHT: CHIFFON IS A POPULAR
SKIRT AND TRAIN FABRIC
BECAUSE IT'S LIGHTWEIGHT
AND SHEER. ALFRED SUNG'S
SILK SATIN SHEATH FEATURES
A CHIFFON TRAIN WITH TRIM
TO MATCH THE DRESS.
ATTACHED AT THE UPPER
BACK, THE TRAIN BILLOWS OUT
BEHIND THE BRIDE LIKE AN
ELABORATE CAPE.

OPPOSITE: THE SILK ORGANZA
BUSTIER BODICE OF THIS
LILA BROUDE CREATION IS
SPRINKLED WITH PEACH AND
GREEN SILK FLOSS EMBROIDERY,
A FRESH, PRETTY SHOT OF
COLOR. THE CIRCULAR SILK
ORGANZA SKIRT CREATES A
SMOOTH, FLOWING CONTRAST.

OPPOSITE: GIVING NEW
MEANING TO THE TERM
"BLUSHING BRIDE," PINK HAS
BECOME A PREMIER WEDDING
DRESS SHADE IN RECENT
SEASONS. VERA WANG WAS AN
EARLY PROPONENT OF PINK,
AND THIS STUNNING ROSE BALL
GOWN WITH BUSTIER BODICE
AND A SKIRT MADE OF LAYERS
AND LAYERS OF PINK AND
WHITE ORGANZA IS JUST ONE
OF HER AMAZING CREATIONS.

LEFT: THIS SATIN JACQUARD
A-LINE GOWN BY SAISON
BLANCHE FEATURES AN
ALLOVER ROSE PATTERN IN
THE FABRIC ITSELF, CREATING
A PRETTY DIMENSIONAL EFFECT.
THE BODICE AND BACK BOW
ARE LIGHTLY BEADED FOR
ADDITIONAL TEXTURE.

Silk crepe is a fabric newly popular with designers; it flows gracefully and smoothly. Tulle is a crisp, netting-like material used for veiling, ball gowns, and underskirts, but organza, a similar material that's a bit lighter and more sheer, is being used in its place more and more, as is chiffon, a thin, transparent silk fabric. Taffeta, another crisp fabric that's often iridescent, is still around, but it's not as common as it was perhaps ten years ago. You may also see dresses with brocade details (raised designs on a heavy jacquard-woven fabric) or velvet used on bodices, cuffs, and hems. For the spring and summer months, you may come across dresses made of linen or even cotton. And believe it or not, wedding dresses have even been created out of leather. Couture, to be sure, but what an entrance that bride would make.

DECEPTIVELY SIMPLE, THIS ALFRED SUNG GOWN FEATURES LACE-AND-BEAD APPLIQUÉS ON ITS EXQUISITE BODICE. SUCH ATTENTION TO DETAIL CAN TRANSFORM A SIMPLE DRESS INTO A WORK OF ART.

THIS SILK ORGANZA BALL GOWN BY RANI FOR ST. PUCCHI SEEMS CUSTOM-MADE FOR A SPRING GARDEN WEDDING. HINTS OF PINK AND GREEN EMBROIDERY ENCIRCLE THE SKIRT AND TRIM THE BODICE, AND A GREEN-GOLD SASH ENDING IN A PRETTY BACK BOW FINISHES THE SUPER-ROMANTIC LOOK.

THE FOCUS OF THIS
PRISCILLA OF BOSTON
SHEATH IS THE ALLOVER
USE OF LACE. A FULL TRAIN
WITH THE SAME ADORNMENT
CREATES THE ILLUSION OF
ADDED FULLNESS. PAIRED WITH
A LACE-EDGED VEIL, THE EFFECT
IS DOWNRIGHT ROMANTIC.

Designers have been using more color in wedding dresses over the past decade than ever before. You can choose pink or rum pink (also known as champagne, it's actually an off-white with just a tinge of blush), peach, blue, even lavender or mint green. Color can come through an underskirt that shows subtly through an organza overskirt, through silk or real flowers on the bodice or back waist of the dress, even in appliqués and blooms sprinkled over the skirt, train, and veil. Dresses done in a period style—Victorian or medieval, for example—often incorporate color in these ways. For a shot of a bold hue, you might choose a wrap in a brilliant color like purple, red, or green for the holidays, or perhaps a floral wrap in pastel shades for spring or summer.

LEFT: A BILLOWING STRAPLESS BALLGOWN OF PURE WHITE SATIN AWAITS ITS BRIDE. SIMPLE DESIGNS SHINE WHEN EXECUTED IN CLEAN, CRISP FABRICS.

OPPOSITE: THIS SOPHISTICATED
WEARKSTATT SHEATH FEATURES
A SILK ORGANZA BACK PANEL
AND FULL TRAIN WITH SILK
FLOWER TRIM. THE MATERIAL,
SILK MIKADO, CREATES A
SMOOTH, SLEEK SILHOUETTE.

LEFT: CREAMY IVORY TURNS
THIS FITTED SHEATH WITH SEXY
FISHTAIL TRAIN AND MATCHING
GLOVES INTO A GLAMOUR-GIRL
GOWN. THE SIMPLE LINES OF
THE GOWN PUT THE FABRIC IN
THE SPOTLIGHT; THE RICH SILK
SATIN NEARLY GLOWS.

Many brides have long dreamed of a traditional white wedding dress, only to dis-
cover that there are actually different shades of white to choose from. They range from
pure white to cream, and you need to try them on to see what best flatters you. If
you try on and fall in love with a dress in a different shade than what you want, be
sure to see a fabric swatch of the color before you order. Here are some guidelines.

Stark white: The brightest, crispest white you'll find, this color looks best
on women with dark complexions. This kind of pure white is achieved best with
synthetic fabrics like satin and taffeta.

RIGHT: OLD-FASHIONED
CROCHETED LACE IS A POPULAR
CHOICE FOR SUMMER BRIDES.
AS A SIMPLE OVERLAY OR
AN ORNATE BODICE, IT ADDS
DIMENSION AND TEXTURE TO
A SIMPLE DRESS.

OPPOSITE: FABRICS CAN BE
MIXED FOR A SUBTLE EFFECT.
LOOK CLOSELY AND YOU'LL SEE
SUBTLE APPLIQUÉS SPRINKLED
ACROSS THE FULL SKIRT OF THIS
PRISCILLA OF BOSTON GOWN.
A BAND OF SATIN AT THE HEM
MATCHES THE BRIDE'S CHIFFON
STOLE, AND PROBABLY HER VEIL
AS WELL.

Silk or natural white: This is the whitest white you can get with natural fibers like silk, and it flatters most skin tones; when in doubt, choose this. It's a shade off stark white, but it will look about the same in photos—and possibly better on you. If your skin has yellow undertones, this is a great shade to try on.

Ivory: Also referred to as eggshell, candlelight, or cream in its various incarnations, the actual shade will vary depending on the fabric. Fairer skin tones look best in yellow ivories; if your skin is not necessarily fair but you do have pink undertones, try creamy colors.

Alfred Sung/Jade Daniels

15 Ingram Drive

Toronto, Ontario M6M 2L7

tel: (212) 397-0882

Amsale

625 Madison Avenue

New York, NY 10022

tel: (800) 765-0170

Ana Hernandez

304 Newbury Street

Suite 411

Boston, MA 02115

Carmela Sutera

226 West 37th Street

5th Floor

New York, NY 10018

tel: (212) 947-1160

Christos

241 West 37th Street

New York, NY 10018

tel: (212) 921-0025

Lila Broude

1375 Broadway

New York, NY 10018

tel: (212) 921-8081

Manalé

260 West 39th Street

11th Floor

New York, NY 10018

tel: (212) 944-6939

Mika Inatome

11 Worth Street

Suite 4B

New York, NY 10013

tel: (212) 966-7777

Priscilla of Boston

40 Cambridge Street

Charlestown, MA 02129

tel: (617) 242-2677

**Saison Blanche/
Eden Glamour**

145 East Walnut Avenue

Monrovia, CA 91016

tel: (781) 853-0615

St. Pucci Bridalwear

2277 Monitor Street

Dallas, TX 75207

tel: (214) 631-4039

Tomasina

615 Washington Road

Pittsburgh, PA 15228-1815

tel: (412) 563-7788

Ulla-Maija

24 West 40th Street

8th Floor

New York, NY 10018

tel: (212) 599-6227

Vera Wang

225 West 39th Street

9th Floor

New York, NY 10018

tel: (800) Vew-Vera

Wearkstatt

33 Green Street

New York, NY 10013

tel: (212) 941-6960

Yumi Katzura

907 Madison Avenue

New York, NY 10022

tel: (212) 772-3760

Photo Credits courtesy of Designers

Amsale: pp. 18, 40, 58, 69

©**Susan Bloche**: p. 39

Lila Broude: pp. 9, 16, 31, 81

Christos: p.68

Corbis: p. 92

Jade Daniels Collection: pp. 27, 63

Eden Bridals: p. 70, 83

Ana Hernandez: pp. 28, 41, 52

©**Lyn Hughes**: pp. 3, 11, 14, 17, 23, 30, 32, 33, 36, 42, 54, 57, 61, 73, 75, 79, 84, 89

Mika Inatome: pp. 35, 47, 53, 72

Yumi Katsura: pp.29

Manalé: pp. 1, 2, 6, 19, 20, 21, 22, 26, 46, 49, 56, 60, 64, 66, 71, 85

Priscilla of Boston: pp. 43, 88, 93

Rani for St. Pucchi: pp. 25, 45, 87

Tony Stone: pp. .24, 38

Alfred Sung: 65, 67, 80, 86

Carmela Sutera: pp. 55, 84

Ulla-Maija: 48, 74, 76, 91

ABOUT THE AUTHOR

Tracy Guth was an associate features editor at *BRIDE'S* magazine and the managing editor of The Knot (www.theknot.com) before striking out on her own as a freelance writer and editor specializing in wedding-related subjects. She has also written and edited for *Good Housekeeping*, *Seventeen*, Beatrice's Web Guide (www.bguide.com) and Astronet (www.astronet.com). Born and raised in Chicago, Tracy now lives and writes in New York City.